Income Taxes for Real Estate Agents

Income Taxes for Real Estate Agents

Published by Desert Mystery Publishing

First print edition published August 2020

Cover art by Mariah Wall
Book layout by Paper Crane Books

ISBN: 978-0-9842205-6-4

Income Taxes for Real Estate Agents

by Amy M. Wall, EA, MBA

This book is dedicated to my beloved husband and editor,
Gary Payne.

Table of Contents

Introduction

SEVERAL YEARS AGO, I HAD an epiphany. I realized that the majority of my clients who owed six figures to the IRS were real estate agents. What a strange coincidence! I thought about it, though, and realized that real estate agents are in the perfect position to get into trouble with their taxes.

1. They tend to be "people" people rather than "numbers" people. After all, they make their living through sales.
2. They have no employer and therefore no tax withholding.
3. Their income is erratic and unpredictable.

No wonder so many of them were in trouble! Full of righteous indignation, I marched into the closest real estate school and demanded to know why they didn't teach real estate agents about income taxes. The owner looked at me hopefully and said, "Do you want to teach a class?"

That was three years ago. On average, I teach 5–7 classes each year, hoping to help keep these fine people out of trouble. At the end of each class, most of them say "I wish I'd known this years ago." This book is the result of three years of teaching and three years of question-and-answer sessions with real estate agents.

The purpose of this book is not to teach you how to prepare your own tax return. I believe that most real estate agents are better off working with a professional tax preparer. Tax laws change constantly—these days, they seem to change weekly. Trying to keep up with all this if you aren't in the tax business is a daunting task. Preparing your own tax return is like FSBO in the real estate world. You know and I know that if you are serious about selling your house, you hire a pro. Similarly, if you are serious about correctly reporting and filing your tax return—and staying out of trouble with the IRS—you get a pro.

What I hope you'll get out of this book is enough knowledge to allow you to make smart business choices, communicate effectively with your tax preparer, and be able to review the prepared tax return for accuracy.

1
You're a Business Owner

IF YOU'RE A REAL ESTATE agent or broker, you're a business owner. As a business owner, you're responsible for paying taxes on your business income. This book will help you understand your obligations: how to calculate your tax, how to minimize your tax, how to pay your tax.

Taxation is a complex subject. Those of us who live in Tax World (a strange alternate reality in which non-real property is a real thing) spend our lives studying it; but I've never met a tax preparer who knows everything. Since it is so complicated, we're going to tackle this subject slowly to give you time to absorb it. Don't expect to skim through this book; please take your time with it.

The first thing to understand is this: as a business owner, you're responsible for understanding some basic business and taxation language. Just as you had to learn special terms to get your real estate license, you must learn some special terms to interact with the other people on your team—like your tax preparer. Most tax preparers do try to "dumb it down" a bit for clients, but we can only take it down so far when it comes to business taxation.

The first bit of business lingo you need to understand is *gross income*. For a real estate agent, your income is generally the amount listed on the 1099-MISC that you get from your broker in January. Occasionally, there are other sources of income, such as payments from other brokers in return for services; that, too, is part of gross income.

The next bit of business lingo you should learn is *net profit*. Net profit is what you get when you subtract all your allowed expenses from your income. Here's the formula:

Gross income - allowed expenses = net profit

So you don't pay tax on the amount listed on that 1099-MISC; you pay tax on the *net profit*. If your gross income is $50,000 and you have $15,000 of allowed expenses, your net profit is $35,000. That's the amount you'll pay tax on. Clearly, allowed expenses are very important; we'll discuss those expenses in Chapter 7.

As a business owner, you must keep track of your income and expenses. People who take their business seriously can tell you, at any given time, what their net income is for the year, how this year compares to last year, and what they expect to "net" (meaning what their net profit will be) by year-end.

When a client tells me they don't know their net profit, I know I'm dealing with an amateur. Note that you can sell a million dollars' worth of real estate and still be an amateur in the "business" of real estate. If you're thinking that you would be happy to be that kind of amateur, let me mention that these are the people who owe six figures to the IRS and will probably spend the rest of their lives trying to pay it off.

2
Taxing Business Income

THERE ARE SEVERAL DIFFERENT TYPES of taxes. The most common is income tax, which applies to income such as interest, ordinary dividends, rental income. There's also a better tax rate for certain types of investment income, such as qualified dividends and long-term capital gain. (The theory behind this better tax rate is that it encourages investment; the reality is that the wealthy people who live on granddaddy's trust fund have managed to snag a better tax rate than the rest of us. Surprise.) And there's FICA tax, also called self-employment tax, also called Social Security tax and Medicare tax. The only type of income subject to self-employment tax is earned income, specifically the type of income earned by W-2 employees and self-employed individuals. Earned income is often called "sweat of the brow income," meaning that people actually had to work to get it. This FICA tax (which stands for Federal Insurance Contributions Act, and no, you don't need to learn that) is about 15.3%. If you are a W-2 employee, your employer pays half and you pay half; if you are self-employed, you pay the full 15.3% yourself *in addition to income tax.* So, if your income tax runs 10%, your total tax rate on your self-employed income is 15.3% + 10% = 25.3%. Your state will also tax you on that income (unless you live in Alaska, Florida, Nevada, South Dakota, Texas, Washington or Wyoming). If it seems like you are paying a lot of tax, you're right.

The one and only saving grace of paying FICA tax is that these taxes are funding your social security account. If you live long enough, you'll eventually get this money back. If you don't, well, thanks for helping fund the pool for the rest of us.

FICA tax is a straight percentage; however, income tax is paid on a sliding scale. A surprising number of people have no idea how income tax works; as a business owner, you need to understand this.

The table on the next page shows the tax brackets for 2020. These rates are applied to *taxable income.* Follow along here.

From the files: Betty and Jim file together for 2020. Betty has a W-2 job and earned $52,400. Jim also has a W-2 job; his income was $42,900. Their combined income is $95,300. Since neither of them are self-employed, we're not worrying about FICA tax in this example. To calculate their taxable income, we take the total income of $95,300 and first subtract their standard deduction of $24,800 (we're assuming they don't have enough deductions to itemize). This results in taxable income of $70,900.

Rate	Single	Married	Head of Household
10%	$0 – $9,875	$0 – $19,750	$0 – $14,100
12%	$9,876 – $40,125	$19,751 – $80,250	$14,101 – $53,700
22%	$40,126 – $85,525	$80,251 – $171,050	$53,701 – $85,500
24%	$85,526 – $163,300	$171,051 – $326,600	$85,501 – $163,300
32%	$163,301 – $207,350	$326,601 – $414,700	$163,301 – $207,350
35%	$207,351 – $518,400	$414,701 – $622,050	$207,351– $518,400
37%	$518,401 and up	$622,051 and up	$518,401 and up

The first $19,750 of taxable income is taxed at 10%, so that's $1,975 of tax. The remaining income of $51,150 ($70,900–$19,750) is taxed at 12%, so that's $6,138. Total income tax is $1,975 + $6,138 = $8,113.

Their *marginal income tax rate* is 12%. Marginal income tax means the highest income tax rate assessed on their income. Their *overall income tax rate* is determined by taking the income tax of $8,113 and dividing it by their total income of $93,500; this is 11.5%.

The effect of the tax brackets is this: even if you make a million dollars, the first $19,750 is only taxed at that 10% rate. And the next chunk up to $80,250 is only taxed at 12%. And so on. I've often heard people say that they don't want to be in a higher tax bracket; this just shows that they don't understand how tax brackets work. Personally, I'd be happy to be in the highest tax bracket. I'd like to pay tax on a million dollars. The tax would be about $298,512, leaving me with $701,488. Marginal tax rate: 37%. Overall tax rate: 29.9%.

3
Business Entities

MOST REAL ESTATE AGENTS START their professional lives as sole proprietors. As sole proprietors, they report their income and expenses on Schedule C, which is filed with their personal tax returns. Many newbies are surprised that they don't have to file a separate tax return for their business. That said, though, certain business entities do have to file separate returns. Read on.

Other business entities that utilize Schedule C, instead of a separate tax return is the LLC (Limited Liability Corporation) and the PLLC (Professional Limited Liability Corporation). In some states, real estate agents are required to form PLLCs rather than LLCs; this requirement comes from the various states' Real Estate Commission organizations. For IRS purposes, a PLLC and an LLC are one and the same. We'll refer to this entity as an LLC, with the understanding that your state may require the creation of a PLLC instead of an LLC.

How does the IRS treat LLCs? As is usual in Tax

World, it depends. LLCs are state-created, rather than federally created, entities. Faced with 50 different versions of a new type of business entity, the IRS made this decision: single member LLCs are treated as sole proprietors. Multi-member LLCs are treated as partnerships. The exception to this is an LLC owned by two spouses in a community property state; in this case, the income and expenses can be split between the two spouses on two separate Schedule Cs.

Partnerships must file a separate and fairly complex tax form called a 1065; the other business entity that files a separate tax return is a sole proprietor or partnership that has elected to be taxed as an Subchapter S Corporation—more on this in Chapter 17.

For now, we'll assume that you, like most real estate agents, are operating as a sole proprietor and will file a Schedule C with your personal return.

4
Setting up the Business

IT'S A VERY GOOD IDEA to keep your business income and expenses separate from your personal income and expenses. This makes the bookkeeping much, much easier. If you form an LLC, there are legal reasons to keep things separate as well. Your business should have its own bank account and its own credit card, if you need to use one.

To get started:

1. Find out if your state requires you to be a PLLC rather than an LLC.
2. Get an Employer Identification Number aka EIN.
3. Set up a bank account for the business.
4. Decide how you'll maintain your records.

An EIN is your business' tax ID number. An EIN is to a business as an SSN is to an individual—it identifies you with the IRS. You can get an EIN completely free of charge at irs.gov; it takes about two minutes to get this. One thing to think about: if you later decide to become an LLC, you'll have to get a new EIN. Consider forming your LLC from the get-go and get your EIN for the LLC. Before making this decision, though, do some research to understand how your state taxes LLCs. Most states don't exact an additional tax on LLCs, but California, Illinois, Massachusetts and Pennsylvania charge additional fees for LLCs. California charges a minimum LLC tax of a whopping $800.

This EIN has another important use. Your broker is required by the IRS to send you a 1099-MISC form each January, reporting your income from the previous year. In order to comply with this requirement, your broker will give you a W-9 form to fill out, asking for your name, address, and tax ID number. If you don't have an EIN, you'll be forced to give your social security number. Under no circumstances should you give your social security number to your broker! Even if you trust the broker, do you trust the office staff? How about the part-timer who comes in during the weekend to help out? Absolutely not—get an EIN and save yourself the worry.

Your bank account will be set up under the EIN. Again, if you don't set up the LLC or PLLC from the get-go and you decide later to set up the LLC or PLLC, then you'll have to get a new EIN. And then have to cancel the previous bank account and get a new one under the new EIN. Not the end of the world, but a bit of a pain in the ass.

Think about how you'll keep track of your income and expenses. Many new real estate agents dash out and purchase a pricey bookkeeping program like QuickBooks. Please don't. Buying QuickBooks for a sole proprietorship with no employees, no inventory and no invoices is like buying a circus tent when all you need is an umbrella.

Really, you can probably get by with a simple spread-sheet, either on-line or on paper. The categories you'll need for this spread sheet are as follows:

- Advertising
- Bank charges
- Cell phone (business use only)
- Client gifts
- Computer repair
- Continuing education
- Dues
- Fees
- Insurance (liability, not health)
- Internet (business use only)
- Meals
- Memberships
- Office supplies
- Open house expenses
- Printing/copying
- Photography
- Repairs
- Signs
- Software
- Suprakey
- Tax prep fees
- New assets purchased

It doesn't need to be more complex than that. We'll discuss these expenses in detail.

5
Introducing the Schedule C

SCHEDULE C (Form 1040 or 1040-SR) Department of the Treasury Internal Revenue Service (99)	**Profit or Loss From Business** (Sole Proprietorship) ► Go to *www.irs.gov/ScheduleC* for instructions and the latest information. ► Attach to Form 1040, 1040-SR, 1040-NR, or 1041; partnerships generally must file Form 1065.	OMB No. 1545-00 20**19** Attachment Sequence No. 09

Name of proprietor — Social security number (SSN)

A	Principal business or profession, including product or service (see instructions)	B Enter code from instructions ►
C	Business name. If no separate business name, leave blank	D Employer ID number (EIN) (see in

E	Business address (including suite or room no.) ► City, town or post office, state, and ZIP code		
F	Accounting method: (1) ☐ Cash (2) ☐ Accrual (3) ☐ Other (specify) ►		
G	Did you "materially participate" in the operation of this business during 2019? If "No," see instructions for limit on losses	☐ Yes	☐
H	If you started or acquired this business during 2019, check here ► ☐		
I	Did you make any payments in 2019 that would require you to file Form(s) 1099? (see instructions)	☐ Yes	☐
J	If "Yes," did you or will you file required Forms 1099?	☐ Yes	☐

YOU'LL FIND BOTH PAGES OF the Schedule C at the end of this chapter. Right now, we'll start at the very the top. It can be confusing for the newbies, so let's review it. Name of proprietor—yep, that's you. Social security number—also you. Business name only needs to be filled in if you actually have a business name, which would be the one you gave the IRS when you got your EIN. That EIN is what goes on line D.

The business address is just your address, unless you have a separate office (your own office that you rent or own, not the desk at your broker's office).

Line B asks for your NAICS (North American Industry Classification System, and now you can forget you ever learned that) business code. This has no effect on your taxes; it just helps the IRS collect information. The business code for real estate agents is 531210. Enter this code in that box.

The accounting method is always going to be Cash for a real estate agent. If you started the business in this tax year, you'll check "YES" for Line G. This does not affect your taxes in any way; this is just information for the IRS.

Lines I and J are a bit tricky. They apply to the filing of Form 1099-MISC (which will be 1099-NEC starting in 2020), which you are required to file if you have paid any non-corporate entity $600 or more in the course of the year. Line I asks if you paid any one person $600 or more in the course of your business during that tax year. Then Line J asks if you filed the correct forms for that payment. Clearly, if you check "YES" on Line I and then "NO" on Line 2, the IRS knows you didn't file forms and will assess a late filing penalty. If you check "NO" on Line I but you really did make such payments, then you've filed a fraudulent tax return. If you check "NO" on Line I and "YES" on Line J, then you didn't understand the questions. If you didn't pay any one person $600 or more in the course of your business during that tax year, then check "NO" and "NO." If you did pay $600 or more in the course of your business during that tax year, make sure to file those 1099-MISC forms and check "YES" and "YES." This applies to monies paid to other real estate agents as well.

You can file 1099 forms yourself by getting the forms from irs.gov or by paying your friendly bookkeeper or tax preparer a nominal fee to file them for you. The 1099-MISC forms ask for *your* information (name, address, EIN, etc.) and then the same for the person who received the money. The IRS' intent, obviously, is to make sure that they know this income was paid out so they can check to see if it was reported on the recipient's tax return. You know your own information; you get the recipient's information by having that person fill out a form called a W-9. Note, please, that the form asks for *your* social security number or EIN. Unless you want the person you paid knowing your social security number, get the EIN and use that number rather than your social security number.

It's important to get that W-9 filled out before you give that person the money. Why? Read on.

From the files: Barbara paid her friend $700 to sit at an open house for her. This would normally be an acceptable business deduction for a real estate agent; however, she hadn't remembered to deal with the 1099-MISC form. She went to her friend and asked her to fill out a W-9 so that we could file the 1099-MISC form (better late than never). The friend refused to fill it out—she didn't want to pay taxes on the income! The result? Barbara didn't want to get caught in the trap of Lines I and J, so she didn't take the deduction. Between her FICA tax and income tax, that little goof cost Barbara close to $200 in additional FICA and income tax. The moral of the story, clearly, is to get that W-9 filled out from the start. If your friend doesn't want to pay tax on it, then find a better friend.

Note that you don't have to fill out a 1099-MISC if the person you paid is a corporation. But the person that you paid $650 for professional photographs of houses? Yes. The editor to whom you paid $700 to write smokin' hot ads? Yes. The housecleaner that you paid $400 to, in order to prepare for an open house? Nope; it's under $600. Businesses will generally supply a W-9 form without a moment's hesitation; they understand the requirements.

If you didn't file a 1099-MISC on time, it's not too late. Late fees vary from $50 per form to $270 per form, depending on how late you are. Intentionally not providing a 1099-MISC form when you were supposed to is subject to a penalty of $550. The IRS takes this seriously; you should as well.

Here's what the W-9 form looks like. It isn't hard to fill out.

W-9

Rev. October 2018
Department of the Treasury
Internal Revenue Service

Request for Taxpayer
Identification Number and Certification

▶ Go to *www.irs.gov/FormW9* for instructions and the latest information.

Give Form to the
requester. Do not
send to the IRS.

1 Name (as shown on your income tax return). Name is required on this line; do not leave this line blank.

2 Business name/disregarded entity name, if different from above

3 Check appropriate box for federal tax classification of the person whose name is entered on line 1. Check only **one** of the following seven boxes.

☐ Individual/sole proprietor or single-member LLC   ☐ C Corporation   ☐ S Corporation   ☐ Partnership   ☐ Trust/estate

☐ Limited liability company. Enter the tax classification (C=C corporation, S=S corporation, P=Partnership) ▶

Note: Check the appropriate box in the line above for the tax classification of the single-member owner. Do not check LLC if the LLC is classified as a single-member LLC that is disregarded from the owner unless the owner of the LLC is another LLC that is **not** disregarded from the owner for U.S. federal tax purposes. Otherwise, a single-member LLC that is disregarded from the owner should check the appropriate box for the tax classification of its owner.

☐ Other (see instructions) ▶

4 Exemptions (codes apply only to certain entities, not individuals; see instructions on page 3).

Exempt payee code (if any)

Exemption from FATCA reporting code (if any)

(Applies to accounts maintained outside the U.S.)

5 Address (number, street, and apt. or suite no.) See instructions.

6 City, state, and ZIP code

Requester's name and address (optional)

7 List account number(s) here (optional)

Part I   Taxpayer Identification Number (TIN)

Enter your TIN in the appropriate box. The TIN provided must match the name given on line 1 to avoid backup withholding. For individuals, this is generally your social security number (SSN). However, for a resident alien, sole proprietor, or disregarded entity, see the instructions for Part I, later. For other entities, it is your employer identification number (EIN). If you do not have a number, see *How to get a TIN*, later.

Note: If the account is in more than one name, see the instructions for line 1. Also see *What Name and Number To Give the Requester* for guidelines on whose number to enter.

Social security number

or

Employer identification number

21

SCHEDULE C
(Form 1040 or 1040-SR)

Department of the Treasury
Internal Revenue Service (99)

Profit or Loss From Business
(Sole Proprietorship)

▶ Go to *www.irs.gov/ScheduleC* for instructions and the latest information.
▶ Attach to Form 1040, 1040-SR, 1040-NR, or 1041; partnerships generally must file Form 1065.

OMB No. 1545-0074

2019

Attachment
Sequence No. **09**

Name of proprietor	Social security number (SSN)

A	Principal business or profession, including product or service (see instructions)	B Enter code from instructions ▶
C	Business name. If no separate business name, leave blank.	D Employer ID number (EIN) (see instr.)
E	Business address (including suite or room no.) ▶	
	City, town or post office, state, and ZIP code	
F	Accounting method: (1) ☐ Cash (2) ☐ Accrual (3) ☐ Other (specify) ▶	
G	Did you "materially participate" in the operation of this business during 2019? If "No," see instructions for limit on losses	☐ Yes ☐ No
H	If you started or acquired this business during 2019, check here ▶ ☐	
I	Did you make any payments in 2019 that would require you to file Form(s) 1099? (see instructions)	☐ Yes ☐ No
J	If "Yes," did you or will you file required Forms 1099?	☐ Yes ☐ No

Part I   Income

1	Gross receipts or sales. See instructions for line 1 and check the box if this income was reported to you on Form W-2 and the "Statutory employee" box on that form was checked . . . . ▶ ☐	1	
2	Returns and allowances	2	
3	Subtract line 2 from line 1	3	
4	Cost of goods sold (from line 42)	4	
5	**Gross profit.** Subtract line 4 from line 3	5	
6	Other income, including federal and state gasoline or fuel tax credit or refund (see instructions)	6	
7	**Gross income.** Add lines 5 and 6 . . . . ▶	7	

Part II   Expenses. Enter expenses for business use of your home **only** on line 30.

8	Advertising	8		18	Office expense (see instructions)	18	
9	Car and truck expenses (see instructions)	9		19	Pension and profit-sharing plans	19	
10	Commissions and fees	10		20	Rent or lease (see instructions):		
11	Contract labor (see instructions)	11		a	Vehicles, machinery, and equipment	20a	
12	Depletion	12		b	Other business property	20b	
13	Depreciation and section 179 expense deduction (not included in Part III) (see instructions)	13		21	Repairs and maintenance	21	
				22	Supplies (not included in Part III)	22	
				23	Taxes and licenses	23	
				24	Travel and meals:		
14	Employee benefit programs (other than on line 19)	14		a	Travel	24a	
15	Insurance (other than health)	15		b	Deductible meals (see instructions)	24b	
16	Interest (see instructions):			25	Utilities	25	
a	Mortgage (paid to banks, etc.)	16a		26	Wages (less employment credits)	26	
b	Other	16b		27a	Other expenses (from line 48)	27a	
17	Legal and professional services	17		b	Reserved for future use	27b	

28	Total expenses before expenses for business use of home. Add lines 8 through 27a . . . . . ▶	28	
29	Tentative profit or (loss). Subtract line 28 from line 7	29	
30	Expenses for business use of your home. Do not report these expenses elsewhere. Attach Form 8829 unless using the simplified method (see instructions). **Simplified method filers only:** enter the total square footage of: (a) your home: _____ and (b) the part of your home used for business: _____. Use the Simplified Method Worksheet in the instructions to figure the amount to enter on line 30	30	
31	Net profit or (loss). Subtract line 30 from line 29. • If a profit, enter on both **Schedule 1 (Form 1040 or 1040-SR), line 3** (or Form 1040-NR, line 13) and on **Schedule SE, line 2** (if you checked the box on line 1, see instructions). Estates and trusts, enter on **Form 1041, line 3.** • If a loss, you must go to line 32.	31	
32	If you have a loss, check the box that describes your investment in this activity (see instructions). • If you checked 32a, enter the loss on both **Schedule 1 (Form 1040 or 1040-SR), line 3** (or Form 1040-NR, line 13) and on **Schedule SE, line 2.** (If you checked the box on line 1, see the line 31 instructions). Estates and trusts, enter on **Form 1041, line 3.** • If you checked 32b, you **must** attach Form 6198. Your loss may be limited.	32a ☐ All investment is at risk 32b ☐ Some investment is not at risk	

For Paperwork Reduction Act Notice, see the separate instructions.   Cat. No. 11334P   Schedule C (Form 1040 or 1040-SR) 2019

INCOME TAXES FOR REAL ESTATE AGENTS

Part III **Cost of Goods Sold** (see instructions)

33 Method(s) used to
value closing inventory: a ☐ Cost   b ☐ Lower of cost or market   c ☐ Other (attach explanation)

34 Was there any change in determining quantities, costs, or valuations between opening and closing inventory?
If "Yes," attach explanation . . . . ☐ Yes   ☐ No

35 Inventory at beginning of year. If different from last year's closing inventory, attach explanation	35	
36 Purchases less cost of items withdrawn for personal use	36	
37 Cost of labor. Do not include any amounts paid to yourself	37	
38 Materials and supplies	38	
39 Other costs	39	
40 Add lines 35 through 39	40	
41 Inventory at end of year	41	
42 **Cost of goods sold.** Subtract line 41 from line 40. Enter the result here and on line 4 .	42	

Part IV **Information on Your Vehicle.** Complete this part **only** if you are claiming car or truck expenses on line 9 and are not required to file Form 4562 for this business. See the instructions for line 13 to find out if you must file Form 4562.

43 When did you place your vehicle in service for business purposes? (month, day, year) ▶ . . . . / . . . . / . . . . . .

44 Of the total number of miles you drove your vehicle during 2019, enter the number of miles you used your vehicle for:

a Business . . . . b Commuting (see instructions) . . . . c Other . . . .

45 Was your vehicle available for personal use during off-duty hours? . . . . ☐ Yes ☐ No

46 Do you (or your spouse) have another vehicle available for personal use? . . . . ☐ Yes ☐ No

47a Do you have evidence to support your deduction? . . . . ☐ Yes ☐ No

b If "Yes," is the evidence written? . . . . ☐ Yes ☐ No

Part V **Other Expenses.** List below business expenses not included on lines 8–26 or line 30.

. . . .	
. . . .	
. . . .	
. . . .	
. . . .	
. . . .	
. . . .	
. . . .	
. . . .	
48 **Total other expenses.** Enter here and on line 27a	48	

6
Income

THE INCOME PORTION OF THE Schedule C isn't as straightforward as you might think. It's not always obvious what Gross Receipts and Sales on Part 1 of the Schedule C means. The number you want to put here is the dollar amount you earned from your real estate business.

	Part I	Income	
1	Gross receipts or sales. See instructions for line 1 and check the box if this income was reported to you on Form W-2 and the "Statutory employee" box on that form was checked ▶ ☐		1
2	Returns and allowances		2
3	Subtract line 2 from line 1		3
4	Cost of goods sold (from line 42)		4
5	**Gross profit.** Subtract line 4 from line 3		5
6	Other income, including federal and state gasoline or fuel tax credit or refund (see instructions)		6
7	**Gross income.** Add lines 5 and 6 ▶		7

It should not include interest earned on your business bank account; that income (that whopping $5 or whatever) properly belongs on Schedule B, with other interest. The reason you want to separate this out is that interest income is taxed differently; it's not subject to the 15.3% FICA tax! Don't add interest to your business income.

Nor should your Gross Receipts and Sales include money you earned from an unrelated business. If you have another business, you should report that on a separate Schedule C. I've had clients with up to four different Schedule Cs for four different businesses. The reason the IRS requires this is simple: they don't want you hiding expenses from an unprofitable business (or worse, a hobby) in with the income from a successful business.

Bill is a successful real estate agent, netting about $55K after expenses. He also is a member of a garage band; I won't use the real name, so let's just call the band the Tucson Turtles. Tucson Turtles makes close to a thousand dollars a year; his share is $250. I didn't know he was combining the garage band income and expenses in with the real estate work until I saw an expense of $2200. Real estate agents rarely spend that much on any single item, so of course I asked what this was. Answer: a drum set. Yes, a new drum set for Tucson Turtles. I insisted on separating out the band's income and expenses from his real estate income and expenses. In the short term, the loss on the garage band was applied against the income on the real estate work, so there was no change to his tax. But eventually the IRS is going to realize that Tucson Turtles is a hobby, not a business. More on hobbies vs. businesses in Chapter 13.

What you list as Gross Receipts and Sales must *always* be at least as much as what the broker's 1099-MISC reported as income. If it isn't, I guarantee that you will get a letter from the IRS asking why you've underreported your income.

Here's something I see a lot: the broker's 1099-MISC is larger than what the real estate agent actually received simply because fees were deducted by the broker, and the agent received the remaining amount. The correct way to handle this is to report the 1099-MISC amount as Gross Receipts and Sales and to deduct the difference as Fees.

You'll see on the Schedule C Income section that there is a line for Returns and Allowances; I can't think of any reason that a real estate agent would have a number there. You also won't have any cost of goods sold, because you are selling services, not goods.

Use the Other Income line to report any other income associated with the real estate business. For example, clients do sometimes give tips or gifts to a particularly helpful agent. A small tip, perhaps $25 worth of movie tickets, would be considered *de minimis* (fancy Latin term meaning "minimal") by the IRS, but something more than that is reportable income. If another agent asked you for help and you were paid for that service, that too would be reportable income. Barter is also considered income. I have yet to come across a situation where a real estate agent bartered services for something else, but I imagine it's possible. In that event, the value of the product or service received is considered income for both bartering parties.

One other thing to remember: if you are handed a check on December 30th, 2019, but don't put it in the bank until January 2nd, 2020, don't kid yourself that you don't have to report the income until 2020. There's this little IRS concept called "constructive receipt." As long as you were in possession of that check in 2019, it's 2019 income. But note that if your broker put the check in the mail on December 30th and included it in your 1099, you're going to need to include that in income even if you didn't receive it until January 3rd. The reason for this is that the IRS is going to go by what the broker's 1099 says. If it is a substantial amount of money, you might want to go back to the broker and try to convince her to send in a corrected 1099.

7
Business Expenses

HERE'S THE MOST INTERESTING PART of the form: Expenses. Remember that Schedule C is used by every sort of small business imaginable, including massage therapists, veterinarians, psychics, bricklayers, steelworkers, and so on. Don't expect to see "Suprakey" or "Open House Expenses" on this form, but that doesn't mean you can't deduct the expense; it just means you have to find a place to list it.

Remember that for an expense to be deductible it must be a reasonable business expense. The language the IRS uses are "ordinary" and "necessary." This is not the time to get creative and out-of-the-box: if the expense in question is not one common to real estate agents, it probably isn't deductible.

Another requirement is that the expense must have actually been paid during the tax year in question. It's not enough to have received the bill; you must have actually *paid* the bill. The exceptions to this are payments made via credit card. As soon as you put the expense on a credit card, it's considered paid (even if it takes you 30 years to pay off the card). But remember that you don't also get to deduct the credit card payments, because you've already deducted the expense. Double-dipping is not allowed in Tax World.

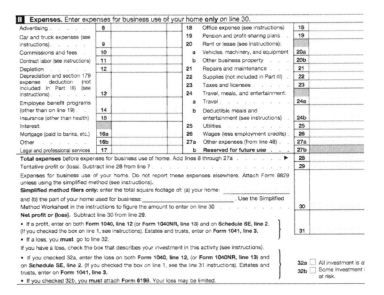

Let's step through the form line by line to see what applies to you:

Advertising. Definitely. This is where you'll record money spent on websites, business cards, yard signs, flyers, banners, whatever has your name on it. Open house expenses can go here as well.

Car and truck expenses. Things get complicated here. Business owners get to choose between deducting a standard mileage rate or deducting a portion of actual expenses. I'll talk a lot more about this in Chapter 10. The number of miles driven for business is entered on the 2nd page of this form; the software does the math, multiplying the number of miles driven by the allowed per mile deduction (57.5 cents in 2020) and bringing that dollar figure to this line. The allowable deduction per mile, aka standard mileage rate, is pegged to the price of gas and varies from year to year. The new rate for the coming year is easily Googled. In addition to the standard mileage rate you can also deduct a portion of the interest on your car loan (not the principal repayment, mind you, just the interest); parking fees and tolls for business trips; and a portion of the personal property tax (lieu tax or auto registration fees) you pay when you register your car each year. Note that some states charge fees based on the weight of the vehicle; these are generally not deductible. The deductible portion depends on how many miles you drove for business vs. how many miles you drove it personally.

Commissions and fees. This is a good place for things like broker fees, MLS fees, membership dues and the like.

Contract labor. This is where you'll record money that you paid for—wait for it—contract laborers. Remember those 1099-MISC forms we talked about? Those costs will go here, as will amounts that you paid to non-employees that weren't high enough ($600) to require filing of a 1099-MISC.

Depletion. Not something you'll ever have to worry about.

Depreciation. Something you might have to worry about. This is a complex subject; see Chapter 8.

Employee benefit programs. A line you probably won't have to deal with. The exception to this is if you hire employees and pay for their health insurance, life insurance, or similar expense. If you hire your spouse and pay for his (and thereby your) health insurance, the cost of that health insurance goes here. See Chapter 11 for more on this.

Insurance. This is where you'll put your E&O premiums, not your health insurance premiums. We'll talk more about health insurance shortly.

Interest. Refers to interest paid specifically for business activities, such as your business credit card and any business loans you might have taken out. Beware of mixing business and personal interest expenses! If you can't reliably sort out business interest from personal interest, the IRS is liable to just disallow the whole mess. If you must use a business credit card, make sure this card is only used for business purposes. If you must take out a business loan, make sure the borrowed funds are used for business only. And no, paying off your personal car loan is not a business purpose. If you are purchasing an office and are paying interest on that loan, that interest could go here. That said, though, it's a bad idea for your real estate business to also own real estate. Talk to an attorney about the legal pitfalls involved.

Legal and professional services. This is where you'll record fees paid to become an LLC, as well as fees paid to your lawyer, bookkeeper and friendly tax preparer.

Office expense. A nice catch-all category. It can include paper, ink, pens, software, even office furniture and equipment that cost less than $2500 each. Put software like Suprakey here as well.

Pension and profit-sharing plans. A line you're unlikely to use, because this line is for employees and NOT repeat NOT for you. We'll talk more about your retirement plans later.

Rent or lease. Here you'll record rent payments if you are renting an office or leasing a piece of office machinery such as a copier. Desk fees paid to the broker can go here as well.

Repairs and maintenance. Where you'll record expenses for computer repairs, as well as repairs and maintenance expenses that are exclusively for your office in home. More on this in Chapter 9, Office in Home.

Supplies. Where you'll record expenses such as staging items.

Taxes and licenses. This is the category that covers your real estate license. Note that the income tax you paid is not deductible and does not go on this line.

Travel and meals. This is a mixed bag. When you take clients out for lunch, you get to deduct 50% of that expense. Don't cut it in half on your own, though—tax software does that math for you. When you stop for lunch on your own there's no deduction even if you had no choice but to eat out. The exception to this is if you are away from what the IRS calls your "tax home" for business purposes. The IRS definition of "away from your tax home" is if you must be away substantially longer than an ordinary's day work. Entertainment is never deductible, not any more. The good old days of deducting country club memberships in order to take the clients out for a round of golf are gone. You also don't get to deduct stuff like your daughter's wedding. Yes, I know you invited a lot of clients to it, but this is not an ordinary and necessary expense.

From the files: Bobbie is a real estate agent who occasionally goes to a rah-rah-real-estate conference in Las Vegas (I'm not totally convinced this isn't just a junket, but whatever) and brings her husband. Her plane ticket is deductible; his is not. Her meals are 50% deductible; his are not. Her hotel room is either 100% deductible or (depending on the auditor) only 50% deductible because she's sharing it. I've seen it go both ways. If the husband had been an employee, then his expenses would have been deductible as well.

From the files: This is a funny story about travel expenses, but not so funny for the client involved. A new client was being audited for a past year return (not filed by my office) for travel expenses. Let's call her Nancy. Nancy showed up at my office with the audit letter in one hand and the tax return in question in the other hand. The tax return showed over $15,000 in travel expenses, highly unlikely in her situation. Nancy said, "There's just no way I spent that much on travel; I just can't figure out where he got that." "He" was, of course, the previous tax preparer, a CPA in California. We called him from my office and very nicely asked him to send over whatever backup documents he had that would explain what was on the tax return. He immediately FAXed over his working papers. Well, Nancy wasn't much on bookkeeping, so what she did was just send him all her bank and credit card statements for that tax year. (She doesn't get away with that half-assed avoidance of responsibility in my office, by the way.) The CPA's staff had done their very best to re-create her income and expenses from these statements. Unfortunately, the CPA's not terribly experienced staff member had seen monthly payments made to a Southwest Airlines credit card and had promptly coded all of these payments as "Travel" because, *obviously*, Southwest Airlines just had to be for travel. Poor Nancy paid the tax, the penalties and the interest. She was gracious enough not to go after the CPA, realizing that she was at fault for a) not providing good information to the CPA and b) not reviewing the tax return before signing it.

Utilities. This covers the utilities in your office, if you have a separate office and pay utilities there. This is also where a portion of your cell phone bill goes. Note that you don't get to deduct 100% of your cell phone bill unless you actually have a separate phone for real estate work. If you only have one cell phone (like most of us) then you can only deduct a portion of the cell phone expense. What percent? That's for you to decide, but it has to be reasonable. If you made $5,000, it's unlikely the IRS will believe that 80% of your cell phone expense was for business. If you made $65K, you might get away with that 80%. If the IRS gets serious about an audit, you might have to provide cell phone records showing how many calls were made for personal reasons and how many calls were made for business reasons. This category is also where you'll put a percentage of your internet cost, if you have an office in home. Again, you don't get to deduct 100% of your internet expense; the IRS is well aware that you play Candy Crush at night.

Wages. This comes into play only if you have actual employees; again—and it just can't be emphasized too much—the owner of a Schedule C sole proprietor business (or LLC or PLLC) is not an employee of that business.

Other expenses. This is the final line in this category. If you flip over to Page 2 of the Schedule C, you'll see that Part V on that page is a list of any expenses that haven't already been captured in Part II on the first page. I prefer to put as many expenses as possible on the first page of Schedule C for the simple reason that I think the return is less likely to get kicked out for review at IRS Central; the IRS software can read the numbers listed in Part V, but not the verbiage; so if a Schedule C comes in with a large portion of its expenses listed in Part V, it would be natural for the computer to kick out the return for someone to look over. And truly, most expenses fit naturally into the Part II categories; I use Part V for continuing education and gifts, but not much else. On the subject of gifts, note that the IRS does not permit a deduction of more than $25 per person per year—and a married couple counts as one person. Yes, I know that you routinely give a large housewarming gift or a beautiful and costly plant, but the IRS has no sympathy. I'm not saying that you shouldn't continue to provide these gifts; I'm just saying that they aren't fully deductible. Many real estate agents put these gifts in as "Advertising" under the theory that the gift card has their name on it. If I were an IRS agent, I'd disallow that simply because you've already sold that client a property and so this marketing piece, aka gift, isn't likely to generate a lead anytime soon.

Notice that you don't see "Clothing" on this form, nor do you see "Beauty Salon" or "Shoes." Yes, I know you have to look good all the time. Yes, I know you spend a fortune on clothes, hair and nails, but it's not deductible. These are personal expenses. The one possible exception here is if you have shirts that have your business name on them.

The cost of said shirts might be considered deductible expenses, but don't get carried away with this. Remember: pigs get slaughtered. (I worked with an accountant who insisted it was "Pigs get fed, hogs get slaughtered," but that's cumbersome.)

You also can't deduct the expenses of *becoming* a real estate agent. The IRS isn't picking on real estate agents in particular; expenses of qualifying for a new career are never deductible. If that weren't the case, we'd all get to deduct our bachelor's and master's degrees, and no one would ever pay tax.

8
Depreciation

TAX WORLD GIVES YOU A way to spread the cost of major assets over time, rather than taking the full amount of the expense all at once. For example, if I buy a new computer for $1,000, I may not need that deduction in the year of purchase. Perhaps I'm expecting more income next year, or fewer deductions. In that situation, I might choose to "depreciate" that computer over time.

This is a judgment call you should discuss with your tax preparer. On one hand, you did spend that $1,000 and would like to reap the tax benefit from that expense. On the other hand, if you expect to be in a higher tax bracket in future years, it makes sense to delay the expense. Remember that taxes should not be regarded as a once-per-lifetime event; planning for the long term is the best approach.

The length of time of depreciation is called class life. Class life is determined by the IRS, not by you. Data equipment (cell phones, laptops, FAX machines, copiers, scanners, etc.) has a 5-year class life. Office furniture has a 7-year class life. The exact amount of depreciation you are allowed is determined by a formula. You don't have to do the math: the tax software does it for you.

In case you're curious, though, the depreciation protocol most commonly used today is called MACRS (Modified Accelerated Cost Recovery System). MACRS uses a half-year convention, meaning that the amount of depreciation you are allowed to take in the first year is cut in half, leaving more depreciation available for future years. Because of this half-year system, five-year property is actually depreciated for 6 years, at the following rates:

Year 1: 20%
Year 2: 32%
Year 3: 19.2%
Year 4: 11.52%
Year 5: 11.52%
Year 6: 5.76%

Our $1,000 computer would be depreciated as follows:

Year 1: $200
Year 2: $320
Year 3: $192
Year 4: $115
Year 5: $116
Year 6: $57

Another easy option is straight line depreciation, which means you'd just divide that $1,000 by 5 and take $200 of expense each year for 5 years.

Note that *mixed-use property*, which is property that is used partly for personal reasons and partly for business reasons, is treated a bit differently, depending on the percent of business use. If that $1,000 computer is used 80% for business and 20% for personal, then you only have $800 of expense to deduct or depreciate. That $800 is called the *depreciable basis*. If you purchase a new cell phone for $600 and it's used 60% for business, you have a depreciable basis of $360.

If you sell a business asset, you may have a taxable event.

From the Files: Cassie had purchased a fancy combo printer/scanner/FAX machine which she used entirely for business. It cost her a whopping $1,500. She elected to take the full expense in the year of purchase, reducing her income by that $1,500. She was happy. Unfortunately, she found the machine too complicated to be useful and sold it the following year on Craigslist for $500. Because she had fully expensed this item, its value in Tax World was zero. When she sold it for $500, she had a $500 taxable gain. Now she was less happy. Had she depreciated it using the MACRS protocol, her depreciation in that first year would only have been $1,500 x 20% = $300. In Tax World, that item would then be worth $1,500 - $300 = $1,200. When she sold it the following year for $500, she would have had a tax-deductible loss of $700.

It doesn't mean it's wrong to fully depreciate the asset and take the deduction in the year of purchase; it just means you should be aware of the possible consequences.

9
Office in Home

ONCE CONSIDERED AN AUDIT RED flag, an office in home, reported on Form 8829, has become a common element of the self-employed tax return.

You're considered to have an office in home if you have an area in your home that's used regularly and exclusively for your real estate activities. *Regular* and *exclusive* are the key words for the IRS. Regular means that you use it regularly, not just once a week. Frequently, not occasionally. Exclusive means that this room or area is not also used for other purposes. It can't also be your bedroom, dining room, kitchen or guest bedroom. Theoretically it could be a part of one of those rooms, but you do run the risk of it being disallowed in the event of an audit.

The ideal office in home is a den or bedroom that has been dedicated entirely to your business. It contains your desk, chair, computer, file cabinets, your Realtor of the Year award, perhaps bookshelves. TV? No. Kid's playpen? No. Guest bed? No.

If you don't have a separate room, but you do have a part of a room that's used for an office, don't count on surviving an audit. Back in 2014, a taxpayer was permitted to take an office in home deduction for a part of her studio apartment. The circumstances were unusual, and you shouldn't assume that an auditor will honor the decision that was made in this case.

If you have your own real estate office—and by this, I mean a real office, not a shared desk in the broker's office—then you won't also get to deduct an office in home. You get to deduct expenses for one or the other, but not both.

There are two different ways of calculating your office in home deduction. First, we have the tried and true method called *actual expenses*. This method utilizes Form 8829. The Form first calculates what percent of your home's square footage is dedicated to your office. In an impossibly simple situation, let's say your office is 200 square feet and the overall house is 2000 square feet. This means that 10% of your qualifying home expenses can be deducted as an office in home expense.

Continuing with our impossibly simple example, let's assume you had these expenses:

Mortgage interest (not principal)	$3,000
Real estate tax	$500
Homeowner's insurance	$500
Gas and electric	$1,300
HOA fees	$1,200

These expenses total $6,500; 10% of that is $650. So far, so good.

Let's say that you had some major repairs done to the house as a whole. You had the roof repaired at a cost of $4,000 and you had the air conditioning fixed at a cost of $1,000. That's another $5,000 of qualifying expenses, meaning another $500 of office in home deduction.

But wait!, as they say on those late-night commercials, there's more. We also get to take a depreciation deduction. Your home office is considered commercial real estate which, by IRS law, is depreciated over 39 years. Here's how that calculation goes:

House purchase price	$220,000
Minus land value	- $20,000
Equals depreciable basis	$200,000

Assuming we're starting depreciation on January 1st (again, this is meant to be an impossibly simple example), we divide the $200,00 by 39 years and arrive at $5,128 per year. 10% of this is $513.

Total office in home deduction:

$$650 + $500 + $513 = $1663.$$

This saves you $254 of FICA tax and, assuming you're in the 12% tax bracket, $200 in federal income tax. You'll also save on state tax, depending on your state's tax bracket.

The wonderful thing about an office in home is that these are all expenses you had whether or not you had a business! You still had to pay the mortgage, the utilities, the HOA fees, etc. Using a home office means you actually get some tax benefit to it.

A few fine points: you don't get any deduction for repairs that didn't affect the home office. Fixed the kitchen faucet? No one cares. Repairs that were 100% for the home office are deducted on Schedule C so that you get 100% of the deduction. Also note that you don't get to deduct water unless you are regularly seeing clients at that office. The fact that you have to pee is a personal problem. Finally, depreciation isn't a free ride. When you eventually sell your principal residence, you will have to *recapture* the depreciation you've taken over the years, aka pay tax on the full amount of depreciation taken over the years as income.

And then there's the simplified method, which is simply the square footage of your office in home multiplied by $5 per square foot, with a cap of $1500. In our example above, that 200 square foot office would net a deduction of $5 x 200 = $1,000. Using actual expenses rather than the simplified method generally gives a better result, but not always. It's worth noting that the simplified method does not include depreciation, so you don't have to recapture depreciation when you sell your home. You also get to deduct the full amount of mortgage interest and real estate tax as an itemized deduction.

By the way, an office in home deduction may not create

or increase a loss; so in the unhappy event that you oper-
ated at a loss that year, you won't be able to take the office
in home deduction. If, however, you utilized the actual
expenses instead of the simplified method, you can carry
that expense forward to the following year.

10
Mileage Expenses

USING A STANDARD MILEAGE RATE to calculate your mileage expense is the easiest way to go, but using actual mileage expenses is still an option. Remember that the standard mileage rate includes the price of gas, repairs, maintenance, depreciation, insurance, etc., pretty much everything except interest on a car loan, vehicle license tax (registration), parking fees and tolls.

If you choose instead to use the actual expense method, you get to deduct some portion of the following:

- Gas and oil
- Repair and maintenance
- Depreciation
- License/registration fees
- Tires
- Insurance
- Car washing
- Auto club dues
- Garage rent
- Lease payments

The portion of these payments that you get to deduct is based on how many miles you drove for business as compared with how many miles you drove in total. If your business miles totaled 10,000 (another impossibly simple example) and the total miles you drove in the year are 30,000, then you get to deduct 1/3 of the above expenses.

Which method is better? Generally, if you are driving a reasonably environmentally conscious car and you put on a lot of miles, the standard mileage rate is a better deal. The good news is that if you use the standard mileage rate for the first year the vehicle was in service, then you get to switch back and forth between actual and standard at your whim; so it's a good idea to start with standard.

But guess what? You have to *actually track your mileage*, which for many real estate agents is like asking pigs to fly. Mileage is a huge deduction for real estate agents (on average 28% of their total deductions) and it's highly audited. Under these circumstances, a rational person would keep careful track of mileage and be audit ready. Stop me if I sound bitter.

There are a number of mileage tracking apps that are ready, willing and able to assist you in tracking your business and personal mileage. The one most of my clients seem to like is called MileIQ. If you just hate phone apps and long for the good old days, feel free to keep a paper log of your miles. I'm betting that by Wednesday, you'll give up and learn how to use your phone. See Chapter 18 to learn how to stay audit ready.

I've mentioned "business miles" several times; let's review what that means. If you don't have an office in home, your first drive of the morning is called *commuting mileage* and is not deductible. You can deduct mileage from your first business stop to your second business step, from your second business stop to your third business stop, etc. But that final drive back home is, again, commuting mileage. Basically, any leg of your journey that starts or ends with a location that is not business related (like your home) is non-deductible mileage. If you do have an office in home, there are no commuting miles, because you basically woke up in your office!

From the files: Jake has five kids, so an office in home just isn't in the cards. He drives from his home to the broker's office (commuting mileage). From the broker's office, he goes to meet clients at an open house (that's deductible business mileage). From there, he drives the clients to several other houses, to lunch, and then back to their car. This is all deductible business mileage. He then drives home (and that's commuting mileage).

From the files: John has only two kids, and there's enough space in his house for an office in home. He drives from his home to the broker's office (deductible business mileage); from the broker's office, he goes to meet clients at an open house (deductible business mileage), then drives the clients to several other houses, to lunch, then back to their car, after which he drives home (all deductible business mileage). See the difference?

Pay attention to the trick questions on Part IV of Schedule C, where the standard mileage is calculated.

Line 43: Where did you place your vehicle in service for business purposes? OK, that's easy enough.

Line 44: Of the total number of miles you drove your vehicle during 2019, enter the number of miles you used your vehicle for:

Business _____Commuting_____Other _____

The only number that means anything on the tax return is the business mileage. The other numbers give the IRS information about whether this is a mixed-use vehicle.

Line 45: Was your vehicle available for personal use during off-duty hours? And you get to check YES or NO. Again, checking to see if this is a mixed-use vehicle.

Line 46: Do you (or your spouse) have another vehicle available for personal use? Again, YES or NO. Now, if you check NO on this one, you'd better also have checked

YES on Line 45. The IRS knows that if you only have one vehicle, it sure was available for personal use and almost certainly was used personally.

Line 47a: Do you have evidence to support your deduction? If you don't have any evidence and you check YES, then you're filing a fraudulent tax return. If you don't have any evidence and you check NO, then you're asking for an audit.

Line 47b: If "Yes," is the evidence written? The IRS considers data storage to be "written." If you checked YES on 47a, you probably should check YES on this one also. Again, remember, this is the IRS giving you the opportunity to hang yourself. Either you're complying with the rules when you check YES and YES, or you are filing a fraudulent tax return. If you check NO on either of Lines 47, then the IRS knows you can't support yourself in an audit.

11
Health Insurance

HEALTH INSURANCE IS A HOT tax topic these days. As a self-employed taxpayer, you don't get to deduct your health insurance from your Schedule C income. You do, however, get to deduct the cost of your health insurance (not to exceed the profit on the business) from your taxable income as an "adjustment." Let's pick that apart a bit. Remember that you pay FICA tax on your Schedule C income, but only income tax on your overall taxable income. It would be nice if you could deduct health insurance on Schedule C in order to reduce both FICA tax and income tax, but no such luck. Instead, you take it as an adjustment, which reduces taxable income but not FICA.

From the files: Sandra is a single taxpayer with no children. Her net Schedule C income (after all expenses were deducted) was $40,000. Her FICA tax is $6,120. She doesn't have enough personal deductions to itemize, so she takes the standard deduction of $12,200 for 2019. She paid $2,000 for health insurance. She gets *adjustments* as follows:

1. Half of the FICA tax, which is $6,120 ÷ 2 = $3,060
2. Health insurance cost = $2,000
Total Adjustments = $5,060

Her income of $40,000 is thus reduced by these adjustments as well as the standard deduction; $40,000 minus $12,200 minus $5,060 = $22,740. She pays FICA tax on the full $40,000 but income tax only on the $22,740.

If you and your spouse get health insurance from an employer on a pre-tax basis, which is common for medium to large employers, then there is no adjustment as described above. The adjustment only works if you are actually paying for health insurance out of pocket.

There is an interesting workaround if you are self-employed and your spouse does not get health insurance from an employer. You can hire your spouse and create a company health insurance plan that pays for the employee's health insurance and his or her family! This workaround allows you to actually deduct the cost of the health insurance from your Schedule C income, meaning that you would pay neither FICA tax nor income tax on the amount you paid for your spouse's health insurance. Note that there has to be a real job (even if it's just answering phones or hammering signs) with a written job description, a real wage, a W-2 filed with the IRS, and a written health insurance plan. You can even take it a step further and set up a health reimbursement plan that pays all your medical expenses out of your business account. Get some help on running the numbers before you sign him up for phone duty, to make sure the savings are worth the hassle and expense of having an employee. Note, though, that you don't have to pay unemployment tax for your spouse, unlike other employees.

While on the subject of hiring family members, note that you can also hire children under 21 years of age without having to pay unemployment tax. If the business is 100% family owned (generally true of sole proprietor real estate agents) then you also don't have to withhold FICA tax on the child's earned income. And it can certainly be helpful to have a millennial on staff.

12
Qualified Business Income Deduction

THE TAX CUTS & JOBS Act of 2017, the least well-thought out and most poorly executed tax change of the past hundred years, added a new deduction for real estate agents (and other businesses, but we're not here to talk about them) for tax years 2018 through 2025.

The deduction can become quite complex, and details are outside the scope of this book; generally speaking, though, the deduction is 20% of qualified business income (QBI), or 20% of taxable income after all adjustments and deductions are subtracted, whichever is less.

There are income limits that phase in if the business in question is a "specified service trade or business." All you need to know is that real estate sales is not a specified service trade or business, so you are not going to be affected by these income limits.

I'm not going to go into all the complexities of this mess; I think a few examples will demonstrate the relevant portions of the deduction.

From the files: Remember Sandra from Chapter 11? Her net business income was $40,000. After adjustments and deductions, her taxable income was $22,740. Her QBI deduction is the *lesser* of 20% of her business income ($40,000 x 20% = $8,000) or 20% of her taxable income after adjustments and deductions ($22,740 x 20% = $4548). The lesser, clearly, is the $4548; so her taxable income is now reduced from $22,740 to $22,740 minus $4548 = $18,192. As you see, her self-employment tax, which is based entirely on her Schedule C net income is not affected; but her income tax is.

From the files: Sarah and John file jointly. Sarah has W-2 wages of $50,000; John's net real estate income is $60,000. They also have interest and dividend income. After adjustments and deductions, their taxable income is $90,000. There is no QBI deduction for wages. John's QBI deduction is, again, the *lesser* of 20% of the net business income ($60,000 x 20% = $12,000) or 20% of the taxable income ($90,000 x 20% = $18,000). In this case, the lesser amount is 20% of John's net business income. And, just to make it a little more interesting, the QBI deduction is reduced by 20% of the adjustments that John gets as a business owner; specifically, the ½ of the self-employment tax that he is allowed to deduct, the health insurance deduction if he takes that, and any retirement contribution deduction that he makes if the retirement contribution is related to his business (a SEP, for example). As I said earlier, it's (overly) complicated.

13
Hobby or Business

WHILE REAL ESTATE AGENTS USUALLY make decent (or even excellent) incomes, it does occasionally happen that an aspiring real estate agent just can't make it work. Perhaps she doesn't have much of a social network, or is shy, or is trying to make a start in a dead market. If the business operates at a loss for several years (possibly as few as 3 years), the IRS could ask the million-dollar question: Is this a business or a hobby?

Why does it matter? Simply this: if it's a hobby, you have to declare the income, but you don't get to deduct the expenses. Unfair? Yep.

The IRS claims that they'll let you take losses for two years out of five. Note that there is nothing hard and fast about this rule. Auditors tell us that the most common reason for a hobby audit is high overall income with a consistent Schedule C loss.

But having losses for several years is definitely a risky position from a tax perspective. The IRS has reason for frowning on repeated losses; after all, you're in business to make money. If the business isn't making money, for whatever reason, why would you continue? And if you really don't care whether you make money or not, chances are good that it's a hobby.

The IRS looks at nine factors when determining whether or not a business enterprise truly qualifies as a business. The nine factors (with my comments in italics) are:

1. The manner in which the taxpayer carries on the activity. *Does the taxpayer keep accurate books? Is there a separate bank account?*

2. The expertise of the taxpayer or his advisers. *Did the taxpayer study the activity's business practices? Were experts consulted?*

3. The time and effort expended by the taxpayer in carrying on the activity. *How much time and effort does the taxpayer expend?*

4. The expectation that the assets used in the activity may appreciate in value. *Will the business assets appreciate, eventually creating a profit?*

5. The success of the taxpayer in carrying on similar or dissimilar activities. *Has the taxpayer been successful in past endeavors?*

6. The taxpayer's history of income or losses with respect to the activity. *Has this activity been profitable for this taxpayer in the past?*

7. The amount of occasional profits. *Even a single year of profits can help prove that this activity is not a hobby.*

8. The financial status of the taxpayer. *Does the taxpayer rely on this business income for living expenses? Or are there other income sources that are being offset by the losses of the activity?*

9. Does the activity lack elements of personal pleasure or recreation? *A large element of personal pleasure may indicate that this is a hobby.*

There have been many, many court cases on this subject; what's clear is that the IRS (or the tax court) makes the decision on a case-by-case basis, looking at each of the nine factors.

If you lose money in the first year of selling real estate, no one will blink. It takes time to build up a clientele. Second year loss? Sure, no problem. Third year? Now we may have questions. A real estate sales business that loses money for several years could be considered a hobby if the agent doesn't operate in a business-like fashion (keeping records, maintaining a separate bank account, etc.); if he doesn't invest much time and energy into it; and if he isn't able to show that he is making changes in order to make a profit.

If your business consistently shows losses and those losses are used to reduce other taxable income, the IRS may start to wonder how it is that you have enough money to live on. The IRS can demand to see bank statements, searching for unreported income. Or they can demand to see receipts for all claimed expenses, searching for unsubstantiated deductions.

Save yourself the grief. Make money, pay taxes. If you really can't make money as a real estate agent after two years of effort, the cosmos is sending you a message: drop it and do something else.

14
Paying Tax

THE IRS HAS A "PAY as you go" policy. This means that they want to be paid as you get paid. If you wait to pay your tax until the end of the year, you may be charged a late payment penalty. Depending on how much you owe, the penalty can be small ($10) or it can be large ($1,000+). If you wish to avoid paying penalties, you'll want to pay tax throughout the year. Note that not all taxpayers want to avoid paying penalties; some say the penalties are worth paying because "I don't want them to have my money one minute sooner than necessary." Yeah, sure, go ahead and pay the penalties if it makes you feel like you're taking a stand, or if you can actually use that money to make more money than what the IRS charges.

You have a few choices as to how to pay your taxes throughout the year. Plan A is to ask your W-2 employee spouse to increase their Federal withholding to cover your tax bill. If you don't have a spouse, or if said spouse is not a W-2 employee, or said spouse thinks you should pay your own bloody taxes, then you have to go to Plan B.

Plan B is to make estimated tax payments on a quarterly basis. These payments are often made with checks accompanied by vouchers called 1040ES forms but can also be made online at irs.gov. The payments aren't actually quarterly—the due dates are April 15th, June 15th, September 15th and January 15th of the following year. These dates vary by a day or two depending on whether or not the 15th falls on a Sunday or holiday.

The tricky part of paying your taxes in advance like this, whether by Plan A or Plan B, is that it's not always easy to predict what your tax is going to be that year. I generally do a mid-year review with my real estate agent clients so we can update their withholding or estimated tax payments, and tell them to come see me in the fall if there's a big jump in income; but even then, large sales at the end of the year can upset the best-laid plans. You may very well end up owing tax. The goal is to avoid paying underpayment penalties in addition to the tax. Generally, you'll have to pay an underpayment penalty if you owe more than $1,000 when you file your tax return.

However, there's a very fine thing called the safe harbor rule. As long as you paid 100% of last year's tax by paying quarterly estimated tax payments or having your employer withhold from your paychecks, you won't pay a penalty. Even if you owe thousands of dollars of tax, there won't be an underpayment penalty. Note that this 100% increases to 110% if you are above the following adjusted gross income limits: $150,000 if you are married filing jointly; $75,000 if you are filing as married filing separately or single.

From the files: George is a single taxpayer who had income tax last year of $9,500. That was his total tax: income tax plus FICA. He had made estimated tax payments of $7,000 and owed $2,500 plus a penalty when he filed his tax return. Pledging not to make the same mistake again, he used the safe harbor rule. His adjusted gross income was over $75,000, so he calculated his safe harbor as follows:

$$\$9,500 + 10\% \text{ of } \$9,500 = \$10,450$$

Spreading these payments out over four equal payments gave him new estimated tax payments of $10,450 ÷ 4 = $2,613 per payment. Even if his income goes up and he owes more tax, he won't have to pay a penalty. Whew!

15
Planning for Retirement

IT'S BEEN SAID A THOUSAND times: the sooner you start saving for retirement, the more likely it is that someday you actually will retire, without having to eat cat food. It isn't easy to save for retirement while still making house payments, raising kids, taking the occasional vacation, and so on. It's so difficult that many people can't accomplish it; millions of elderly Americans live in poverty. It sucks to be old; it sucks to be in poor health; but imagine being old, in poor health and dirt poor. That vision should spur you to action.

There are many retirement savings vehicles; social security is probably the most widely known (and utilized) of the lot. Of course, the Big Concern of all my younger readers is: "It probably won't be around when I get old enough to take it." I don't blame them for harboring that suspicion. I thought the same for most of my life; I'm now 65 years old, and it's looking pretty good. While Social Security may not look quite the same 20 years from now, it's unlikely to disappear completely; it's just too important to too many voters.

Social security pools mandatory contributions from workers into a large bucket; then it pays out benefits to those who have contributed and who have lived long enough to benefit. In order to be eligible for Social Security benefits, you must earn enough "credits" during your working years. In 2020, you'll receive one credit for every $1,360 in earnings, up to a maximum of four credits per year. The amount required to earn a quarter increases each year. You don't lose the credits if you switch jobs or take a break from work; these credits stay with you no matter what. You need 40 credits, or 10 years of work, to qualify for retirement benefits. This does not mean that after ten years of work you get to retire; the minimum age to collect social security is 62. However, if your full retirement age is 67 and you decide to start at 62, then you'll get just 70% of the amount you'd be eligible for at 67. On the other hand, every year you wait to collect increases your payout by 8%, maximizing at age 70.

Social security was never meant to supply your full retirement needs. The way financial advisors figure it is this: your post-retirement expenses will be about 70–80% of your pre-retirement expenses. There are a few reasons for this: you are now on Medicare, so your medical expenses will drop; you don't need work clothes, you don't need to put as much mileage on your car, hopefully your house is paid off, etc. This isn't figuring in round-the-world cruises, clearly. However, social security will usually cover only about 40% of your pre-retirement income. This means you'll need to get that remaining 30% from savings. And that's where retirement planning comes in.

This is a complex subject and you should discuss your particular situation with your tax professional, but here's a quick overview of the top choices:

1. Traditional IRA: Contributing to a traditional IRA is, for most people, tax deductible. This means that if your overall tax rate is 22% bracket and you contribute $1,000, you'll save $220 in tax that year plus savings in state tax. The contribution limit for 2020 is $6,000 with an additional "catch-up contribution" of $1,000 available for those 50 or older. You must have earned income of at least the amount of your contribution in order to make that contribution. Also, there are potential income limits; check in with your tax professional. This is a very easy account to set up; any bank or financial institution will be happy to help you. Withdrawals are subject to tax when withdrawn; the idea is that when you are retired, you'll be in a lower tax bracket.

2. Roth IRA: This is similar to a traditional IRA in terms of contribution limits, but it isn't tax-deductible. That's the bad news. The good news is that it isn't taxed when you take it out if you're at least 59 ½ years old. This is a good choice for people who don't expect their tax brackets to go down in the future. Again, easy to set up with any bank or financial institution.

3. Solo 401(k): This plan allows you to contribute a great deal more money to your retirement account. As of 2020, the contribution limit maxed out at $57,000 plus an additional catch-up contribution of $6,500 for those who are 50 or older, or 100% of earned income, whichever is less. If you have a Subchapter S Corporation, you can contribute as both an employee and as an employer. As an employee, you can contribute the full 100% of compensation (for 2020 not to exceed $19,500 plus $6,500 catch-up if you are over 50 years of age). As the employer, you can contribute an additional 25% of compensation. Special rule for sole proprietors and single member LLCs: you can contribute 25% of net self-employment, defined in this case as net profit less half your self-employment tax and plan contributions. The Solo 401(k) involves a little more paperwork than the IRA, Roth IRA or SEP IRA, so don't go this route unless you really are able to make the extra contributions. Note: If you have an S Corp and you have employees other than a spouse, you cannot have a Solo 401(k).

4. SEP IRA: SEPs allow for contributions only by the employer, not the employee. If you are self-employed, meaning you are not filing as an S Corp, the contribution limit is 25% of your net income on your Schedule C, not to exceed $57,000 for 2020. If you have employees, you must contribute an equal percentage of salary for each eligible employee. If you contribute 10% of compensation for yourself, you must also contribute 10% for the other employees as well.

5. SIMPLE IRA: The contribution limit is $13,500 in 2020, plus a catch-up contribution of $3,000 if you are 50 or older. Employees can contribute via salary deferral, and employers are generally required to make matching or fixed contributions. This can be an expensive way to go if you have a large number of employees, but this is rarely a concern for a real estate agent.

Most real estate agents I've worked with who have Subchapter S Corporations go for the SEP IRA plan. Contributions are due by the tax-filing deadline (April 15th) or by the extension deadline (October 15th). Again, it's definitely worthwhile to meet with a retirement planner to help make sure you've selected the plan that's right for you.

16
E-filing and Tax Deadlines

ELECTRONIC FILING CAME INTO BEING in 1986 when 5 tax preparers from Cincinnati, Raleigh, Durham and Phoenix were part of a test program. Prior to that time, tax returns were filled out by hand and sent in by mail. Today, e-filing, as we call it, is standard practice.

I still occasionally have a client who wants to file a paper return. My response is something like this: "Paper returns have to be input into the IRS computers by minimum wage employees who may or may not input the data correctly, but hey, I'll print it out for you to mail in if that's what you want." And that usually results in "Oh, no, I didn't realize, please do e-file it." Contrarily, it sometimes happens that someone wants to e-file but can't because someone has stolen their identity and has already filed. Or because the ex-spouse who wasn't supposed to claim the child as a dependent did so anyway, so now you have to paper-file and let the IRS decide which of you is right. Or because what you think your last name is doesn't match what the IRS thinks your last name is (often a problem for people who have hyphenated or complex last names).

Bottom line: if you can e-file, do so. That way the IRS has a correct tax return in the data base.

Due dates were fairly consistent until 2020. The dates shown below are pre-2020 dates and also, very likely, post-2020 dates. Typically, personal tax returns—including Schedule C forms—are due on April 15th of each calendar year for the prior tax year. This date can be off by a day or two if April 15th falls on a weekend or a holiday. You're allowed to file an extension that extends that deadline by six months, making your deadline October 15th—again, plus a day or two if that date falls on a weekend or a holiday. Note, however, that an extension of that filing time does not extend the PAYMENT time! Obviously, if that wasn't the case, we'd all file extensions so that we could keep our money for six extra months! I mean, seriously—DUH.

Now, this is confusing—how can you pay your taxes if you haven't filed? And the answer is that you must sort of, kind of, prepare your taxes. You have to do a "best guess." If that best guess shows that you're going to owe money, then you should send that amount of money in with the extension. Does it sometimes happen that your best guess was wrong, and you owe money anyway? Yes, of course. But if you've at least sent some money in, then your interest and penalties are reduced.

Weirdly and stupidly, the first estimated tax payment for the current year is also due on April 15th. Let's say you filed your 2019 tax return on time and owed $4,000 on that tax return. That $4,000 is supposed to be paid by April 15th, 2020. Your tax preparer, correctly, also sets you up with estimated tax payments of $1,000 per quarter in order to cover your expected 2020 taxes. What does that mean? It means that not only do you owe $4,000 from 2019 on April 15th, 2020—you also owe that first $1,000 for your 2020 taxes on that same date. Does that suck? Yes, absolutely. And guess what? A mere two months later, on June 15th, you'll owe another $1,000 for your 2020 taxes. Yep, the first half of the calendar year is tough for the self-employed.

17
Subchapter S Corporations

I'VE MENTIONED SUBCHAPTER S CORPORATIONS briefly; a Subchapter S Corporation (hereafter referred to as S Corp) is a type of business entity. Other business entities are sole proprietorships, partnerships, and C Corporations.

A typical scenario for a real estate agent is to start as a sole proprietor—or as an LLC, though single member LLCs are taxed as sole proprietors—and then decide to be taxed as an S Corporation. In Tax World, we call this "making the S election." This is done by filling out and mailing in Form 2553. I recommend having your tax preparer make the election for you, but if you're bound and determined to do it yourself, read the instructions. And then you'll probably decide to have your tax preparer do it.

The great benefit to functioning as an S Corp is that not all of your income is subject to self-employment tax. Whereas the sole proprietor pays both income tax and self-employment tax on all income, the S Corp shareholder pays income tax on all net income, but self-employment tax only on a portion of the income.

Let's take a step back. When the sole proprietor "makes the S election," he creates a new entity: the S Corp. He then becomes an employee of the S Corp. He gets a salary, and the IRS rule is that this salary has to be reasonable compensation for the work he does. The remaining income, if there is any, is treated as corporate distributions.

What does this mean in Tax World? It means that the salary is subject to both income tax and self-employment tax, while the corporate distributions are subject to income tax, *but not self-employment tax*. Depending on how much the corporate distributions are, the savings in tax is either insignificant or quite large.

Let's look at a few examples.

From the files: Anne set up an S Corporation. Her net income for the year (remember this means gross income minus expenses) is $60,000. Over the course of the year, she has taken a salary of $50,000 and distributions of $10,000. Her tax savings are equal to the FICA tax she didn't have to pay on those distributions. FICA tax is 15.3%, so her savings are approximately $10,000 x .153 = $1500. This is not an exact calculation, but it makes the point.

From the files: Darren set up an S Corporation. His net income for the year was $45,000. There wasn't enough income for him to also take distributions, so there is no tax savings.

From the files: Bob set up an S Corporation. His net income for the year was $100,000. Over the course of the year, he has taken a salary of $50,000 and distributions of $50,000. His tax savings are equal to the FICA tax he didn't have to pay on those distributions. FICA tax is 15.3%, so his tax savings is roughly $50,000 x .153 = $7,500. Again, this is not an exact number, but you get the idea.

So why wouldn't everyone set up an S Corps, just in case there's enough income to get distributions? Because there are expenses involved in running an S Corporation. First, there's the cost of the S Corporation tax return. S Corps get their very own tax return, and these tend to not be cheap. Second, you have to pay someone to help you do payroll. I beg you not to think you can do this on your own; it's more complicated than you think. Also, if your time isn't worth more than the $35 per hour you'll pay someone to do the work, then you aren't ready to utilize an S Corp. Third, because you are an employee, you have to pay unemployment tax on your wages. Typically, I don't set up an S Corp for any business owner until they're netting at least $60K per year with the expectation of earning at least that much every year moving forward.

There's another aspect to this. There is a higher degree of self-discipline involved in terms of how you handle your business accounts. It isn't for everyone, as—frankly—not everyone has the brains and/or discipline to successfully run an S Corp. Please be realistic about your abilities. If you're not highly disciplined, if you're not willing to act like a real business owner (rather than just a salesperson), then this isn't for you.

I'm not going to teach you how to work with an S Corporation in this book. It's complicated. If you think you qualify for an S Corporation, find a tax preparer and get corroboration on your opinion. Get a quote on the preparation of the tax return and ask what sort of support you can expect to receive throughout the year in terms of adjusting your payroll, withholding, etc.

18
Audits

THE IRS STILL DOES AUDIT people, but there aren't a lot of audits. In 2018 the IRS audited less than 1% of all individual returns. Most of these audits were conducted by mail, not in person. Here's how to increase your chances of being audited:

1. Don't report all your income. Nothing gets the IRS' attention faster than not accounting for all your W-2s and 1099s, or reporting less income than what those forms show.

2. Make a lot of money. Your odds of being audited go up as your income goes up.

3. Take higher than average deductions, particularly charitable contributions and medical expenses.

4. File a Schedule C (yep, that's you). Particularly if you

make a lot of money or show a lot of deductions, Schedule C tends to attract audits. If you file a Schedule C and show income of over $200,000, your audit rate goes up to 1.4%.

5. File Schedule C showing losses for multiple years. This definitely applies to those kinda-sorta real estate agents who renew their license, take classes, etc., but somehow never actually make any money.

6. Take big deductions for meals and travel on Schedule C. And yes, that can definitely apply to real estate agents.

7. Claim 100% business use for a vehicle. You may as well put a sign on your front yard saying, "IRS agent enter here." The IRS knows full well that you're using that same car to take your kids to school, stop in at the grocery store, etc.

8. Claim large rental losses. The IRS actively scrutinizes large rental real estate losses.

9. Fail to report gambling winnings.

10. Engage in virtual currency transactions.

11. Fail to report a foreign bank account.

All in all, the Schedule C is the most heavily audited form by the IRS. The deductions most likely to catch the attention of the IRS? Meals, travel, mileage, gifts, office in home. This doesn't mean that you shouldn't take the deduction; it means that you should make sure your documentation is in order. If you can't document it, don't deduct it.

Also, remember that pigs get slaughtered. If you earned $10K in real estate and spent $3K on meals, that's more than just stupid. It's downright piggish. And thus highly auditable.

19

Working with Your Tax Preparer

As you've seen from this book, taxes are complicated. While it's important that you, as the business owner, understand your tax situation, there's no substitute for having a competent and willing-to-help tax preparer on your business team. Don't just pick the first tax preparer who pops up on your Google search! Ask fellow real estate agents (successful ones) for a recommendation. Interview a few preparers until you find someone you're comfortable with.

First, make sure your tax preparer has the proper credentials. Fly-by-night tax preparers are everywhere, making a quick buck and disappearing. You need someone who has a license to protect, who is required to take continuing education every year, and who will be available to you year-round. There are two credentials that I recommend. An Enrolled Agent is an income tax specialist, licensed by the IRS after passing a rigorous three-part exam that's entirely about income taxes: Individual Taxation; Business Taxation;

Representation, Practice and Procedures. Alternately, a CPA (Certified Public Accountant) has a degree in accounting and has passed a difficult four-part test covering these aspects of accounting: Auditing & Attestation; Financial Accounting & Reporting; Regulation; and Business Environment & Concepts. Note that you don't see Income Tax here—there are CPAs who do no tax work at all, but most do. They are licensed by their state of residence. Both Enrolled Agents and CPAs have "rights" with the IRS, specifically the right to represent taxpayers in tax disputes.

Second, make sure your tax preparer is familiar with small business taxation. Not all credentialed preparers do business work; some specialize in individual returns, others in estates and trusts. It's reasonable, during the interview process, to inquire as to how much small business experience your potential preparer has. Also inquire as to whether or not this potential preparer has experience with the preparation of S Corp returns. I've seen real estate agents who could have saved thousands of dollars utilizing the S Corp option but who were talked out of it by preparers who just didn't want to have to do the S Corp return.

Third, your potential tax preparer must be willing to answer questions as they come up for you during the year. Unless you are really getting out of hand, there should not be a charge for answering your questions. If you get charged for your questions, you'll be reluctant to ask them; if you're reluctant to ask them, you're going to make mistakes; if you make mistakes, you'll be mad at the tax preparer. As long as you are not abusing your tax preparer's time, questions should be encouraged.

Fourth, the tax preparer must be willing to do a mid-year review at no cost, or for a minimal fee. I build the cost of the review into the preparation fee; that way the real estate agent feels entitled to the review—which is exactly what I want.

You have responsibilities in this relationship as well.

First, present your income and expenses in a clear and concise format. If your tax preparer has a worksheet for you, use it. It's *your responsibility* to convey your income and expenses accurately. Do not, ever, EVER, bring in a tub full of receipts unless the tax preparer has agreed to this ahead of time. (And, frankly, I'd be suspicious of a tax preparer who has the time to monkey around with this sort of nonsense during tax season.) Paperwork is part of the job description. If you're just no good at bookkeeping, hire someone who is. If you can't do it yourself and refuse to hire someone to do it, then you should go work for someone else and get a W-2.

Second, answer the preparer's questions as promptly as possible. When we can't get an answer to a question quickly, we close your file and move on to someone else's file. No worries, though; we'll get back to your file. Eventually.

Third, be respectful of your preparer's time. Many clients don't realize that preparers have ten weeks in which to earn their income for the entire year; if a client misses an appointment with little or no notice, that's a wasted hour.

In my practice, I let that happen once; the second time, I write a sad little letter explaining that they are not a good fit for my practice.

20
Closing Thoughts

IT'S BEEN MY GREAT PLEASURE to work with many, many real estate agents over the years. I've watched some fail; I've watched others succeed beyond their wildest expectations. The successful agents seem to have no commonality in terms of gender, race, education, or socioeconomic origins, but they do have certain traits in common:

1. They treat real estate sales as a real business, not as a side gig.
2. They put money aside for the inevitable market downturns.
3. They pay attention to business details.
4. They know their strengths and weaknesses in terms of business; they team up with other professionals to support those weaknesses.
5. They meet problems head-on rather than avoid them.
6. They invest in their business.

7. They stay current in terms of social media and new ways of connecting with people.
8. They care about their clients.
9. They are personable but not pushovers.
10. They look and sound like professionals.

I wish you the best of luck in your real estate endeavors. Taxes are a pain, but staying on top of that aspect of your business frees you up to go do what you love: selling real estate!

Disclaimer

This booklet is intended as a general commentary taxation for real estate agents. It is not intended to represent tax law, nor is it intended to apply to any reader's particular tax situation. It is no substitute for the advice of your own tax professional. As an IRS Circular 230 practitioner, I have no responsibility for any positions you take on your tax return, unless I have prepared and signed that tax return. For a detailed analysis of your tax situation, please consult your tax advisor.

Made in the USA
Monee, IL
25 May 2021